THE OUT-OF-BODY SHOP

Praise for The Out-of-Body Shop

Whether homing in on the "blank, bright/as black lacquer" eye of a dead bird, the "scavenger-scattered/cryptic ghost script across the snow," or the fireflies she mistakes for the father's materialized threat "to burn// every single weed/into the goddam dirt," Mitchell leaves no shade of grief or beauty unexamined. Rigorously crafted, these emotionally evocative poems probe what lies below veneers, beyond smoke screens, beneath the relentless pull of memories. They wrestle with the paradox of being at once "in the body, but not/of the body" and release their energy like the sacred "lit/sweet grass/braid" mourners pass hand-to-hand at a friend's burial ceremony. *The Out-of-Body Shop* is transfixing and transformative.
　　　　　—Mihaela Moscaluic, author of *Immigrant Model*

Drifting tantalizingly between the vivid, piercing particularity of personal memory and the unanchored intimacy of philosophical reflection, *The Out-of-Body Shop* bridges the distance between body and mind and reminds the reader that to be human is to live, always, in the vibrant space between. Nancy Mitchell is a high priestess of the art, and this book is not to be missed.
　　　　　—Alexandra Kleeman, author of *You Too Can Have a Body Like Mine*

Nancy Mitchell has written a book of ghosts, of family long and recently gone, of friends, both the actual dead and those lost (as yet) merely to distance and our myriad contemporary distractions. "We like one another," Mitchell says, "we have emojis."—This rare yoking of irony and true feeling is shot through the book. The poems too are ghosts, partial and startling, often leaving the reader with a single, primary color feeling, melded to sensory detail. As in the poem, "Ghost Smoke," where the poet is wakened in the middle of the night by the smell of cigarette smoke. Though not entirely awake, and no one in the house has smoked for years, the poet recognizes the scent—it's the brand her dead mother favored, "Ginny Skinnies, she called them." These are the poems of a romantic all grown up, a lover who has broken through successive layers of illusion and now entertains the visitations of romance, in all its forms, as a sober adult. Such romance is no longer limited to the realm of bodily experience, and the book ranges through events of the past and the present with egalitarian ease. After reading thorough these skillful, haunted (and haunting) poems, one realizes the aptness of the title: the book itself is an "Out-of-Body Shop," where the soul is no longer constrained by time and space, and goes where it must for healing, restitution, and love.

—JEFFREY SKINNER, author of *Chance Divine*

Nancy Mitchell's tour-de-force *The Out-of-Body Shop* looks into the "unbearable lightness of being" and does not flinch. The Southern Gothic landscape of her familial history is filled with ghosts that have followed into the present moment remembering, along with the poems, the bodily split of human trauma. Mitchell's poems illustrate the great Truth that "the retro-fit of the body depends on remembering—." This highly anticipated third volume illustrates how, exactly, the otherworldly resides within us and outside of us right inside the tender lyric, blooming of things. "The Out-of-Body Shop" is the place we all come to to be born a new, piece by piece, the long letting go that is the sun shining in through the kitchen window in morning.

—ELIZABETH POWELL, author of *Willy Loman's Reckless Daughter*

Making use of wide-ranging poetic strategies, from jagged, consonant-filled lyrics to gothic Frost-like narratives, Nancy Mitchell tells a startling story of a woman's survival. In the course of this journey she mercilessly moves through and beyond the pain and grief of damaged, impoverished family life, transforming her speaker's powerlessness to a state of grace, a humane hope in the possibility of change.

—IRA SADOFF

THE OUT-OF-BODY
SHOP

Nancy Mitchell

a plume editions book

AN IMPRINT OF MADHAT PRESS

ASHEVILLE, NORTH CAROLINA

MadHat Press
MadHat Incorporated
PO Box 8364, Asheville, NC 28814

The Library of Congress has assigned
this edition a Control Number of
2018945750

ISBN 978-1-941196-71-7 (paperback)

Text by Nancy Mitchell
Author photo by Alyssa Maloof
Cover image by Richard Carter
Cover design by Marc Vincenz

Plume Editions
an imprint of MadHat Press
www.MadHat-Press.com

First Printing

For John, who cleared the path,
for Dzvinia, who held the light

Table of Contents

... the key no longer turns in the lock
Of the mysterious door of bodies.

—Robert Desnos, *Awakenings*

The Past

If we have to bring it
up, we'll need gloves—

latex pulled elbow-
high, a mask—gas—safety

glasses. We'll take it
outside, spread the decades

in the sun, burn
off the mold, the stink.

Nancy Mitchell

Prudence

To come upon ivy
creeping a path
turns fire in the heart

to ash in the mouth.
Wheat sprouted
from seeds sown

in an oak's shadow
will be mottled
with stripe blight.

Cow milk pailed
in a copper bucket
turns blue if stirred

with a silver spoon.
To meet a drunkard
before dawn will undo

the curse of the ghost
owl's who-hoot,
as does dirt twice

spit on by a liar and split
with an idle rust-
dulled trowel.

To make fertile
a field lain seven
years fallow, stir

sow-blood into mare-
dung with a hickory
ladle, then batten

for a fortnight with gander
feathers. At dogwood
bloom it should be flung

over the left shoulder
of a blindfolded widower.
Know far troubles

loom like the harvest
moon. Small as a star
near troubles are.

Nancy Mitchell

Unbearable

after Milan Kundera

Want to make love
outdoors and eat dark
bread knock out
this wall with a sledge-
hammer and let the night
in sink my arms in warm
mud all the way up
to my elbows swim
in the black river
that runs through the city—
all night, under water

Intake Invoice

Triggering Secondary
Incident: Female. Fifth grade.
School bus driver—grandfatherly, smelled
of soap and rising dough.
Called her *chica*
bonita, asked about books
she liked. His hand—
blue veins, skin thin
as tracing paper—slid
up her blouse, callused
edge of his thumb nicking
her nipple. *The whole time*
he was smiling. Typical
symptoms: lightness
of being, sense of shrinking.

Exit Point: black hole
in his eye. *God*
Hole she called it.
Static: Yes.
Time Out elapsed: Unknown

Nancy Mitchell

The Out-of-Body-Shop

Slipped on ice
      in the grocery store
      parking lot
         and rose

            like a helium party

balloon
        constellation of oranges against black

      asphalt ringing
       my fallen body

passersby rally like ants
           around a scattered picnic

I float in a blizzard of static

              embryonic

      trailing a cut

umbilical cord

      I have
        no idea   how long

           in sound-booth silence

Catatonic Snow White

newyorker.com/magazine/2017/04/03/the-trauma-of-facing-deportation

Body feels as it is entirely liquid.
Limbs soft and porous. Unable
to get out of bed. A turning
toward the wall and pounding
fists. Can't eat, swallowing
impossible. Deep pressure in brain
and ears as if underwater in a diving
bell. Significant, sudden weight
loss. Reflexes intact. Pulse and blood
pressure normal. Wrists lifted a few
inches fall when dropped. No response
to claps or whispers, strokes
to the cheek with a feather.

Nancy Mitchell

Family Photograph, circa 1920

Of the four sisters in my grandparent's brood
of ten, I loved Helen best. Not baby

Louise cuddled in her mother's lap, bright
with the beauty that would later earn her

the Tobacco Princess crown. Not smoky
teenage Esther, whom I was said to favor.

Not even my mother Marie, fading
at twenty. It was Helen, dark hair combed

back from her plain, rigid-as-a-soldier's
face, unsoftened by a single curl. Only Helen

in black, the neck of her dress buttoned tight.
I'd stand on my parent's bed and touch each

pale oval. The six brothers' heads rose
from dark suits and floated against the backdrop

of darker curtains. The sisters' faces flowered
on long white necks. My finger would find its way

back to linger on Helen—the one I loved
the most because I knew she was loved the least.

Farewell to Bellehaven

1912

Azaleas blazed on Aunt Norfleet's wedding day.
Bridesmaids' whispers mingled with the swish
of crinoline slips ... *Irving ... not deserving,*

*rough at the edges, drinks too much. But, did come
from old money ... was known clear to Asheville
for fair and square dealings in tobacco.*

Before Norfleet's daddy gave her away
he dabbed his eyes, and squinted through her lace
veil: *don't you forget the blood you come from.*

1913

Spring, a year later, *the blood she come from*
crossed the street at the First Methodist church,
where a jealous drunk, idling in his pickup,

mistook Mamma for his wife and Daddy
for her lover. He gunned his truck and struck
them dead, corner of Magnolia and Main.

1914–1919

Thereafter, at the first forsythia
sprig, Norfleet took to her bed and stayed until
the May Beau, her one and only, was born.

9

With just the pickaninnies on the farm
for playmates, Beau talked just like them. School kids
curled their tongues to make big lips and mocked

him something fierce until one Sunday
after church he flung a jug of kerosene
onto the dying embers in the parlor

fireplace. Jarred from his nap by the blast,
Irving found his son out cold on his back
his legs flaming like hickory kindling.

1920–1922

Doctors grafted skin until it took. Scab
patches itched like chiggers and stung like lard
splatter, but not as bad as the schoolyard

taunts, and Beau swore never to go
back. Five days after his hospital release,
weak as a litter runt and white as biscuit

dough he jumped from the back of a tobacco
truck hell-bent down the farm to market road
to broken legs and a shattered hip.

Norfleet eased his tedious months in traction
by reading aloud from *Great Expectations,*
swirling their favorite passages with stars.

1939

Norfleet homeschooled Beau into Duke—tuition
paid by the last ninety acres of hardwood
razed for a pine plantation—where he stayed

for half of September then came back
home to hole up in his room until over
the oak rope-bed (where everyone knew

but only the kitchen help said) *he done*
hung himself dead after Irving had caught
him needling morphine with a negress.

1967

At eighty-two Irving plugs cotton balls
into keyholes—*to keep the ghosts out*—
while he's not snitching from the whiskey

behind the leather-bound *Lee's Lieutenants*
on his great-granddaddy's desk—custom made,
ebony-inlaid mahogany, shipped

from London to New Orleans, 1870.
Hauled back to Bellehaven in a mule-driven
flat-bed by the freed field hand sent to fetch it.

Norfleet hangs above the desk, shoulders fogged
with pink chiffon, pearls studding her neck, a deb,
five years before she met Irving and all

11

the troubles ensued. Her fox-head stole lies
coiled in her lap, its beady eyes shiny
as wood ticks, as if it already knew.

Ice clinking against whiskey tumblers chime
through the night. The tattered lace curtain
flutters in the breeze like an empty sleeve.

Would-Have-Been Mother-in-Law Overheard at the DAR Tea

… not to mention Mother's mother's
diamond ring Mother passed
to me when she passed

and I passed to my son to give
his fiancée … not to mention the trouble
of fixing up the carriage house

behind her folks' place where they'd
stay just until he graduated
and got back on his feet … not

to mention the bridesmaid dresses
so expensive her mother's
own Irish lace gown altered to fit

her tiny hips waiting in cold
storage where he left the note on her hope
chest—*you deserve better*

… not to mention … what a shame …. what—
this cup is chipped and what is this
red all over my napkin?

Nancy Mitchell

What Were Fireflies

Five, maybe I was
six, out on the back

stoop about to first-star
wish when the Queen

Anne's lace in the empty
lot next door lit up with what

I thought was my dad's
butane torch, him all liquored

up, finally making good
on his threat to *burn*

*every single weed
into the goddam dirt.*

Ah in Father

wanton wanderer
   squander quandary

daughter qualm
   fog bother

   ah! dah! farther god, farther

Nancy Mitchell

Never the Same After

that day in the grocery store
when my mother, who

seconds before had nodded
absently to my nattering

for ice cream, pushed back
the blond wave streaming

from her widow's peak,
looked up from her shopping

list and smiled as if we'd just met,
rested her hand light as a white church

glove on my arm and whispered
Little girl, I think it's time

for you to go back home.
This from she who had forbidden

me to cross the cul-de-sac without
a grown-up. As if I had some

other mother looking out
the window of another house

waiting for me. And she,
this woman now touching me,

had, for all my life, only
been playing make-believe.

Nancy Mitchell

Then

Pond ripples ran alongside her
until she heard it was water

blown by wind. When the dog
next door panted, she believed

it grinned. Bubbles in the bathtub
drain were fish eyes—evidence

of the sea heaving beneath
her feet. For proof her mother

would live until Easter, she asked
for a red bird and behold! on the branch

two appeared. Her mother's spirit
summer fog then. Before she knew.

Work

With the flex of an uncle's corporate muscle, I was interviewed by a squat, cigarillo-smoking plant manager. I'd applied for the only summer position in a small appliance factory in job-strapped eastern North Carolina. Ignoring my outstretched hand, she gave me the once-over, nodded and said *Plastics*. I giggled and winked, certain she alluded to the famous one-liner to Dustin Hoffman in *The Graduate*. Through blown smoke she shot me a stink-eye and smacked the paper-clipped edge of my application against her metal desk. *Graveyard shift,* she spat, *start tonight.*

While my friends partied and slept, I sweated next to a steel behemoth as it heaved its belly full of molten plastic into molds. I pulled blender bodies into the fluorescent swamp-bile of factory air. Fiery threads seared my arms. Cradled in thick oven mitts, it was passed to the sander and buffer and plastic wrapper, an assembly line of women who could trace a lineage as straight as the stick up a Daughter of the American Revolution's ass to the slave shacks of the plantation whose remaining ten acres lay a mile away.

Twice a shift the machine rested, ticking off our fifteen-minute breaks. We poured our shared pouch of peanuts into Pepsi bottles and watched them bloat in the fizz. Between pinches of snuff, the women would take turns parceling out wisdom: *See yonder fork lifter? used to be sniffing up every skirt, and he ain't looked at you once ... it ain't because you're ugly—'cept for that pimple on your chin. Why? his woman done wove her curly hair around his zipper.* They'd nod and cluck, take a swig of Pepsi and scan the floor for more examples.

See Miss Supervisor's red hair? ... she was 'got when her mama was on the bleed ... don't you laugh now! To my amazed face they'd shake their heads. *I'll swan-nee ... why, you as dumb as a hickory stump ...*

that pimple on your chin? ... you ain't letting your boyfriend into your panties. I touched my chin and wondered how they knew. The sander leaned in and hissed *You 'fraid once he done get it, he done gone ... well, listen here ... make him up some tomato soup for lunch ... and stir in a teaspoon of your bleed, and he won't never leave you.* When I recoiled in disgust they'd slap their knees, pinch some snuff, nudge each other and cackle. Rolling their eyes and nodding their heads, they agreed that *Miss Uppity ... is going on off to college with a head stuffed full of nuthin'.*

Night after night my mind was blown. At each shift's end, I'd pull the tight nylon net from my head and shake my hair out in the dank morning air. I'd drive home through low fog, the screech of metal against metal still dinning my ears as the wind whipped the funk of burnt plastic back in my face.

Erstwhile Brood Hen Farmer Laments

for Rick Bland

For a roost I used the empty old corn
crib on the two acres with the tenant
shack I rented and cobbled together
a sorry row of boxes and stuffed them
with straw. Outside of that I didn't know
exactly what to do with the five hens
and rooster from the farm store but
scatter feed and put water in a pie
pan, especially when they flew up
into the trees to sleep. My landlord Jess
gave me the stink-eye for not knowing
about flight feathers—he cut them
with his wife's kitchen scissors. For a while
it was fun to get up early like a real farmer
and check for eggs although they never
did lay more than a few, and I was scared
of the rooster after that bastard
pecked the hell out of my leg. But I was
a bad steward—be gone for days
to see the Dead, never thinking
their water would dry up, or be stoned
on Acapulco Gold and forget to latch
the gate. My dog got in and left a mess
of feathers, blood and chicken shit.
I tasted rust. I kicked him, then cried
until I puked. When Jess drove in
and saw just the two hens huddling
in the corner, he never came back
except for the rent which I taped

to the door so the wind wouldn't
take it. At night I tell the wind
if I had another chance I'd raise
that brood better.

It's No Fox

or else you'd see the drag
trail into the woods and nothing
left save a few feathers

it's a skunk that sucks
the blood out, leaves the body
to rot—damn if that hen

don't look like she just lay
down to sleep, her neck
blood-stuck with feed.

Nancy Mitchell

Vespers

iPhone, light
my hand to a pen

or a pill, split ticket
to sleep: drawn

birds, quarter
curtain, no clock.

Praise

You be my Sunday
morning hot

butter-swirled
syrup-drizzled

whipped-cream-
dollop-topped

hand-scratch-made
pancake.

I be your coffee cup,
Starbucked.

Summer without Mercy

I was certain the backlit, distinctly female silhouette I saw through the glass panel of his front door was a shadow flickering across the dark foyer. Certain, until he opened the door and stuck his neck out to say, as if I were a fucking Jehovah's Witness, *This just isn't a good time.*

His *sorry you had to find out this way ... ok if I swing by to pick up my things?* on my voice mail. The next day, I had my phone number and door locks changed. Friends rallied like ants around a dropped crumb, swept me up and out to dinner. With each *he's a jerk ... doesn't deserve you ... forget him ... you'll find someone better* I felt a rage rise like bile, until one friend put her hand on mine and leaned in with *at least you didn't find him in flagrante delicto.* The others tittered. I folded my napkin carefully, and into their faces mouthed *Fuck You* and walked five miles home through the darkest streets I knew. My circle of friends shrank to a noose.

I ignored my beloved gardenia's hot white blooms, was unmoved by their heady perfume. I stopped watering them and watched them slowly wither and die. I turned my back on poetry, refused its lame consolations, scorned the arc and resolution. All summer I lay with my pain, sustained it with a two-minute loop of perfected misery: the woman's shadow, then his face at the door, his voice. Pain was my edge against evaporating into the ether of numbed grace after Dickinson's "great pain." Pain my ballast against the inevitable gravitation pull into the "stupor," the penultimate stage before the final letting go.

Then, Again

She teased, and gently tugged his silver
tufts of ear hair, new, ten years later. Laughing,

he straddled her and traced the crow's feet and wrinkles
on her cheek where she had been lying

across his chest. They watched tree branches
lengthen on the ceiling, and tried remembering

all the phone booths they'd snuck off
to—pockets so heavy with change—

and called each other from back
then. Drifting between kisses

they might have fallen
asleep, except that he kept jerking

up and going to the window
to check on his car illegally parked.

Their gray morning swirled flurries.
He paced, fretting if the worn tires

would be safe, if he'd be able to see
the road ahead, if he'd get back

home before his wife, before
it really started coming down.

Nancy Mitchell

Ashes

Shifted in the box
like sand riddled
with small stones—

bone that would not
burn swirled water
like smoke gusted

away by wind—
what mote now
and in what eye?

How Reckoned

O toad, O blue-eyed
    doe, O silver fox head

smirking—Spirits! Is she yet
    worthy, fit to sit

among you—she with the white
    horse's breath warm

and steady between
    her breasts—her mother's

ashes still smoldering
    in one hand?

Ghost Smoke

My husband loathes the smell and wouldn't
marry me until I quit. Fifteen years
now and if he catches even a whiff of a fugitive
wisp in my hair, he refuses to touch me
unless I wash it out. Into our smoking guests' hands
he presses clamshell ashtrays and shoos them off
to smoke on our dock on the lake.

Mornings after a party, the fog not yet lifted,
I'll see him kneeling in his black bathrobe
to fish out their flicked filters bobbing
like miniature buoys along the shoreline.

I was surprised when the smell woke only
me. Shielding his eyes, I turned on the light,
and could find no signs of smoke or track
a trace beyond the bedroom. For weeks after
I'd smell it at random times. When it woke
me again last night, I couldn't get back
to sleep, so I flipped around
on TV until I landed on a BBC special
interview of those claiming visitations
from their beloved deceased.

A young lawyer testified that garlic,
freshly split and grated onto a cutting board,
was her grandmother along on the traffic-
snarled drives to work, particularly
during a big trial. Punctuating with an arthritic
finger, an elderly man vouched that *beyond a doubt*
his late wife wafted lilies while he lay with his head

encased in an MRI tube. A pierced-lipped teen
lisped a *swear to frigging god* his father—dropped
dead this past Christmas—soothed his nightmare-
jagged sleep in a mist of Old Spice.

Haunting me all day to the extent that I forgot
to buy gin for martinis was the suspicion that the smell
which woke me was smoke from my late mother's Virginia
Slims, or *Ginny Skinnies* as she called them. Yes, the mornings
it would wind its way up the stairs twenty minutes
before she'd *rise and shine* us out of bed. That
and the staccato of tap water hitting
the copper kettle bottom were the only signs
she was up. Her feet, our family joked,
never touched the floor, in contrast to our father's
window-shuddering tread—her warning
to douse her cigarette and turn
on the stove's exhaust fan.

Likewise, at his shoe thud on the first stair
riser my sister would quickly spritz
our room with Aqua Net while I stubbed
out our cigarettes—pilfered from Mother's stash
hidden in a Kotex box—then flicked
them out the window where butts littered
the porch roof below like pigeon dung.
By the time our father, flushed
and huffing, flung open the door, my sister
and I would raise our kohl-smoked eyes
in surprise from the glossy pages of *Seventeen*.

To say this was not the visitation
I had hoped for would be ungrateful. Mother
took care to be scrupulously fair, but how
can this compare to my sister's account
of being roused from sleep by gentle
strokes on her cheek to behold my mother 's
face, smooth of worry lines, haloed by blond
billows of Lauren Bacall hair? Smiling,
she kissed my sister's forehead, then floated
off into the night on a pink cloud of chiffon
nightgown, trailing a wake of Chanel No.5

But no. The smell was my mother—smoke
from her mornings alone, smoking
as she waited for the kettle to sing
steam into the dark
kitchen, smoking
as she watched her face
vanish in the windowpane
as the sky lightened, smoking
as was her wish, smoking
as was her wont, smoking her only
do as I damn well please.

Field

By day a body of water
out a window.

Come evening
blackout drapes
rain-stained sleep.

By morning
every dream redacted.

Nancy Mitchell

Why I'm Here

I have no clue—it was weird, yes
but I would say *molested* but
not *abused* like the one
here who was raped
repeatedly and caged or that one
chained four hundred days to a radiator …

But, the technicians insist (*in layman's
terms*) there is always the initial,
primal, if you will, incident, after
which the connection to the body
is intrinsically damaged—think
electrical cord, think frayed—
it's the culmination of subsequent,
less significant incidents that cause
the final, often irreparable, split.

We all here want, hope, to be fixed—
but chances of a successful retrofit
to the body depend
on remembering—
most cases are too far
gone—the damage.

While in the Body

I was in the body, but not
of the body. I neither

grew nor aged—
an alabaster egg.

Under a furled rib
cage like a lover

I spooned the heart,
and bided my time

counting beats
to the lullaby—

arterial freeway,
traffic of blood.

The One I Called

Urged to a new life on eastern shore town in the middle of an August heat wave thirty years ago, I fled my marriage of fifteen years. I took up in a townhouse within a walk from the small college upon which John Barth had cast a jaundiced gleam of fame in *The End of the Road*. With the influence of well-established friends, my three heathen children were enrolled in a Catholic school. I accepted a position teaching English competency to students deadheaded to eight-hour rubber-boots-on-blood-slicked-concrete shifts processing chickens for Frank Perdue. One month in, driving into the path of a Mack truck filled with these chickens presented itself as a perfectly sane and brilliant alternative.

One very late night, exhausted, I fell to my knees to look out the low open bedroom window. To a full moon silvering the dumpster, to the crickets chipping away last remnants of summer, to the sea-salted breeze I prayed for help, for relief from the illegible essays pillaring my desk, overflowing laundry hampers and the kid-worries spinning my gut. Nothing could persuade my third-grader to put his hand to anything other than slowly rolling a pencil up and down his desk (a session with the priest had been scheduled), or stop my daughter's sobbing that no one in fifth grade ever picked her for kickball, or distract my thirteen-year-old from exploring etching possibilities of a sharp sewing needle on his arm. "Fool!" the husband had shouted after me, and fool I was. I had not counted the cost; I could not do it. But I had to do it; I could not go back and we had to eat.

The following yellow-leaf-lit October evening, the good angel floated into the last poem of a mutual friend's reading, trailing the belt of his stained trench coat. Leaning on the wall next to the door I'd chosen the chair closest to for a quick exit, he blew steam from a Styrofoam cup. During the applause, as I moved to slip out, he turned; my shoulder bumped his hand and a wave of warm coffee broke against my collar bone, splattered my white dress. After a flurried exchange of *So sorry, no, my fault ... No, it's my fault, I should have ...* he attempted to blot my dress with the hem of his coat, stopping short at my breasts. Then introductions, sticky handshakes, and his accepted offer to walk me home.

At an AA meeting; third one today was why he was late, and I didn't flinch. Our mutual friend had given me a sketch: newly, shakily sober, flush with an NEA he was free to housesit while this friend and his wife would be in Greece during an upcoming sabbatical.

His breath was an elixir of stale coffee, cigarettes, and peppermint; when he leaned in for a kiss I couldn't resist.

The wise ones caution the newly sober and newly separated against "embarking" on a relationship for at least a year. In our defense, rather than embark we simply drifted; my bed our boat, the night our dark sea becalmed by my sleeping children's breath. My only thought of the future was where he'd next put his lips.

And so it went; under the shelter of his wings we dwelt; between loads of laundry he wrote and swept; my kids and I came home to a clean house, warm fish sticks and pizza. When my ex showed up drunk, swinging an enormous gourd and bellowing obscenities on my doorstep, the good angel led us out the back door to a neighbor's house where he called the police, then a cab to take us to a movie.

The townhouse rules forbade four-legged pets, so he gave the kids Porgy and Bess, parakeets who flew now and then about the house, until through an open door they slipped, above and beyond the kids' tearful pleas. If I'd known anything about the nature of angels, I would have seen this as an omen. Maybe he took off to answer the call of a more urgent prayer, or perhaps his work with us was done. By the lowly prod of rote and repetition I'd pushed my students through the bureaucratic loophole to graduation; my kids finished the school year with decent grades, played with friends on softball teams and swam happily in the pool. It was June.

Black Bittern

Always reacted bad to happy—crushed it
when I could like a lame bird gimping
under my work boot—at two I chucked
a metal Tonka truck into the TV
to shut my sister's singing to Big Bird
on *Sesame Street*—drove my fists into the cake
my mom made for my birthday—a tiny
silver plane pulled my name in blue
cursive across a fluffy field of white
icing—goddamn, her face—too much pretty
and I'd shake with rage, had to smash

things up. Bad tooth abscess at 13—oxycontin
for the pain—and lo and fucking behold
it tamped the demon down—drove that beast
into a cave, kept it at bay—but the price
for peace a man is made to pay—gerbil wheel
of scoringdealingjailrehab—ring of ink
roped 'round my neck for every year—but
what the fuck—my last bid in the big house
and the fits just quit—got out, stayed clean, went

to AA, Tech for welding degree—met
Katie and bam! the kid—I could finally
breathe. Until today, my birthday—came to camp
out by the river—and there's Katie, our baby
at her tit, back lit with some goddamn golden
shaft of light beaming through the pin oak trees—
and I could feel the old gear ratchet up
in my guts and I was itching to hit
something—the hatchet heavy in my hand

from splitting firewood. Said I had to piss—
then dove for the double dose of gray death
and works stashed up under the truck bumper.

Had to—when my boy was born I put one
hand on his head, the other on my heart
and swore if I ever had just one thought
of hurting him, I'd do myself in then
and there. So—here I am—hunkered down
on a tree stump, sunk in the stink of river
muck and reeds. When the tide turns I'll punch

the needle in—by the time I'm good and gone
the rough, rogue current will sweep me clean
away—and my sweet fucking Katie-girl
back at that picnic table with the cake,
the candles waiting to be lit. I guess

the sole witness to the one and only vow
I've ever made, much less kept, is that black
bittern above, circling back to her nest.

Friends Here

All we are now
is floating text
next to a thumbnail
of the body
we left. We reminisce
on all the ways a warm
body feels against
another body, how
voices sound
so differently in fog
than in the dark
and day and everything
the smell of rain
changes. We try
not to complain
about the constant ache
and to be grateful:
we like each other;
we have emojis.

Tijuana Alternative

for Rick Maloof, 1942–2010

1.

While nurses smudged your temples
with holy dirt dug from chapel gardens
and hovered reiki hands like dark
clouds above kidneys, your wife
trolled her laptop for statistics:
black graphs of stage-four
survival-rate percentages.

As you sweated in eucalyptus
saunas, she combed the maze of gang-
graffitied streets for a fabric store, grit
under her sandal strap rubbing
a blister she wouldn't feel until
she lay down next to you that night.

Lina—linen she whispered
to the salesgirl's head bent to texting,
a crucifix glinting in the shadowed
cleft between her breasts. She nodded
toward a shelf, but when your wife said
Por una mortaja, shroud, the girl
brought Jesus to her lips.

2.

She bought the twenty feet of white
linen the *How to Wrap a Body for Burial*
website advised. Hid it in a duffle bag
before the two of you flew home to snow

so deep six friends in hip boots had to pull
you from the taxi on a kayak makeshifted
as a sled. Before poultices of wild roots
and mint infusions were applied, chimes

rung to quicken chakras, before the friends
and family came and stayed and needed
to be fed, circled your bed chanting, holding
hands in prayer. And she prayed too, but

the only kind of miracles she'd seen
were like how the dead fawn in the woods
last fall—body still warm, coat not
not yet stiff, eyes a deep well

of black ink—in just two months
had become a brambled nest
of bones scavenger-scattered
in a ghost script across the snow.

Nancy Mitchell

Pickaxe Dawn

Your wife gave us each a small brass
bell to *please ring* as we followed

her to the bare-branched copse of oak
sheltering the small grove your son

at dawn pickaxed frozen ground
to dig a small hole for your ashes.

Ring, please keep ringing, as our twenty
boot-heels beat a mud path through old

snow and cornstalk stubble, *ringing keep
ringing* around the collapsed barn

ringing rubble of cedar shakes, snarled
bramble of barbed wire *ringing*

all along the *ringing* river shivering
beside us, *ringing* red-winged

blackbirds from the blackberry
thicket until your *ringing* grandson,

four, threw his bell, monkey-hear-no-
evil hands over his *ringing* ears, screaming.

Ceremony

Into the small hole your wife poured a stream
of ashes, then dropped the pair of dog tags

that clinked your slog through napalm fog then hung
two decades from your Saab's rear-view mirror.

Unstrung beads from Belize slipped your daughter's fingers
like blue glass seeds while your son let fly a clutch

of red hawk, owl and osprey feathers scavenged
on walks with you along the river. We who could sing

sang *Amazing Grace,* and passed a lit sweet-grass
braid, its wispy wreath wrapping us.

Nancy Mitchell

Obituary

Shot of scotch, hit
of weed mostly stems

and seeds. Is that fog
stalled on the pond

or smoke? And the farther
geese—flung ash, and
the nearer, cinders?

There, on the dock—a heron
folding into itself, or is it

a blown newspaper
split, your face halved?

Grace Notes

Is that doleful song a cardinal's
or the clock's battery wearing down?

Said she'd try to meet him for a drink.
but the cat curls so warmly at her hip,

the tea has just cooled enough
to sip, the laptop sits so squarely

in her lap, and there out the window,
what bird is it that doesn't fly

upward so much as is lifted
to the branch by an invisible hand?

Easier to find a four-leaf clover
in a nettle patch than linen pants

on line for him—*no, not yellow,*
more a goldenrod—

36 waist, he can have them
taken in if he gets thinner.

There's no finding him shirts, too,
only *blue just this side of sea breeze*

as anything else will wash him out,
and *please, no three-quarter sleeves.*

Like the rusted hinge of the picket
fence, wings of passing geese creak.

Is their falling shit the velocity
of snow or rain or leaf?

Pines cast shadows; further
from noon, longer the reach.

What sense, now, in getting dressed
up, eyeliner, lipstick, without which

she's plainer than a marsh hen.
How the Kleenex wads flock

at her feet like small sheep grazing
the carpet. It's Philip Glass in her ear

buds again, smearing the greens,
blurring the hours clean.

Eye

Blank. Bright
black lacquer—
I thought the bird

had fallen
from the wreath,
then saw the raindrop

of red against white.
Its tuft, spiked,
a dried paintbrush.

Its left socket—
swarming, a blood-
fest of gnats.

Nancy Mitchell

Riders of the Squall

Howls buffered by storm windows, we slept
while those punks lobbed pollen bombs hazing

the driveway in yellow fog then spiked
pinecone grenades in new sod. And for spite

spit sticky red sap against the white fence
wet with paint, and snapped the ornamental

maple sapling in half, as rogues ravaged
the rhododendrons, pink petals littering

the black mulch like tickertape confetti.
Hooligan hurricane gusts hijacked the canoe

and flew it to shatter the nest we'd watched
the pair of geese weave. River reeds, ivy,

and down feathers—bunting plucked from her own
breast—now blasted bits eddy-swirled.

Driving Past Our Married House

Ivy you trained those twenty years along
the trellis has run up to our old second-story

bedroom window. Gutters you slipped
on the wet roof and broke your arm

to clean—even after I warned you
not to after the third drink—now choke

on muck of pine needle and maple leaf.
Oh, your beloved boxwoods—green fists

you planted when our son was three, grown
to his waist at seventeen—now list like

drunks, spindly and brown
like an apple rotted from the inside out.

You got such a kick out of telling our friends
again and again what the cable guy said, brushing

cobwebs from his hair after he'd belly-crawled
the attic floor to lay the line for our new TV:

damned if this is not the tightest house I've ever seen
How proud you were, how you'd beam.

Nancy Mitchell

Prayers Reversed

You come back. Dishes dirty
themselves and pile the sink;
closets open and clothes

fling themselves like wives
on husbands' funeral pyres
to the floor in a heap. Our son

throws a punch, daughter screams
bloody. Toast burns and the air
stinks of the cigar smoke rising

from behind the business
report you're reading. Slowly
I gather the car keys, my purse,

passports, our will and good
silver. Shush the children,
lure them with Peeps

from the TV's gleam before
we slip out the back door
careful of the hinge's creak.

Leaving

a scatter of shore lights
as seen from a boat

its rope slipped
to the last knuckled knot

sail luffing—rag tatter
yawing into dark

a fallen galaxy

ACKNOWLEDGEMENTS

Grateful acknowledgments to the editors of the following print and online publications in which these poems, some in earlier versions and under different titles, originally appeared.

Bending Genres: "Black Bittern."

Big Muddy: "Farewell to Bellehaven" (originally titled "Bellehaven Summer, 1967"); "While in the Body" (originally titled "When a Soul").

Columbia River Review: "Leaving" (originally titled "Fallen Galaxy"); "Never the Same After"; "Then, Again" (originally titled "Then Again, Some Ten Years Later"); "The Past."

Connotation Press: "Ashes"; "Praise."

Euphony: "Vespers" (originally titled "Moonlight, 3 AM").

Green Mountains Review: "Driving Past Our Marriage House"; "Grace Notes"; "Tijuana Alternative"; "Would-Have-Been Mother-in-Law Overheard at the DAR Tea."

Louisville Review: "Family Photograph, circa 1920."

Rise Up Review: "Catatonic Snow White" (originally titled "Sleeping Beauty Syndrome").

Plume: "Ghost Smoke"; "Summer Without Mercy"; "The One I Called"; "Unbearable"; "Why I'm Here"; "Work."

The Plume Anthology of Poetry 3: "It's No Fox"; "What Were Fireflies."

The Plume Anthology of Poetry 4: "Obituary."

The Plume Anthology of Poetry 5: "Erstwhile Brood Hen Farmer Laments"

The Plume Anthology of Poetry 6: "Prayers Reversed."

Solstice Literary Magazine: "Pickaxe Dawn" (originally titled "Ringing").

Superstition Review: "The Out-of-Body Shop"; "Intake Invoice."

Tar River Review: "Riders of the Squall" (originally titled "Night Vandals"); "Prudence."

The Northern Virginia Review: "Eye" (originally titled "If Not for the Blood").

Thrush: "How Reckoned."

Tulane Review: "Then."

Valparaiso Poetry Review: "Ceremony."

Washington Square Review: "Ah in Father."

"Grace Notes" was reprinted in *The Pushcart Prize XXXVI* (2012).

Deepest gratitude to editors Danny Lawless and Marc Vincenz for their faith in this collection and to F. J. Bergmann for invaluable assistance in "retrofitting" this manuscript for this out-of-body shop; to Adam Tavel for unstinting editorial support and encouragement; to Dzvinia Orlowsky, my first reader and midwife to many of these poems; to Michael Waters and Michaela Moscaluic for enduring friendship and solid editorial advice; to Jean Valentine for our abiding ebb and flow; to Kelly Rouse and Teresa Bland for their unwavering support; to Virginia Center for the Creative Arts for a residency at Le Moulin à Nef; to Oregon State University for a residency at the Cabin at Shotpouch Creek. For keeping this body tethered to this sweet world, endless gratitude to my children Zac Mitchell, Sara Irving and her children, Seth Mitchell, his wife Julie Oh and their children, and finally and always to my husband John Ebert.

About the Author

NANCY MITCHELL is the author of *The Near Surround* (Four Way Books, 2002) and *Grief Hut* (Cervena Barva Press, 2009), and with Daniel Lawless co-edited *Plume Interviews I* (MadHat Inc., 2017). Her poems have appeared in a wide variety of journals and are anthologized in *Last Call* (Sarabande Books, 2000); *The Working Poet: 75 Writing Exercises and a Poetry Anthology* (Autumn House Press, 2009) and *The Plume Poetry Anthologies* 3, 4, 5 & 6. Mitchell is a 2012 Pushcart Prize winner and serves as Associate Editor of Special Features for *Plume*. She lives on the eastern shore of Maryland with her husband John Ebert and teaches at Salisbury University.